A Church Walls

The Local Church—
World Facing and World Affirming

Mike Lowe

Vicar, All Saints, Marple, Diocese of Chester

GROVE BOOKS LIMITED
RIDLEY HALL RD CAMBRIDGE CB3 9HU

Contents

1. Into the Community 3
2. Vision and Planting 7
3. Strategic Outreach 12
4. A Theological Reflection 16

Acknowledgements

I wish to express my appreciation to all my brothers and sisters at All Saints, St Paul's, and Cross Lane Fellowship. I would like to especially thank Jean for typing the manuscript.

Prologue

Humpty Dumpty sat on the wall
Humpty Dumpty had a great fall
All the King's horses and
All the King's men
Couldn't put Humpty together again.

The fall of Humpty Dumpty is well reported
and the fact that no-one could help
is clearly a tragedy.

The Sovereign's subjects, both animal
and human, failed in this attempt of assistance.
The King's concern is represented
by the attempts of his subjects.

Was Humpty Dumpty a member of his local church?
Was Humpty Dumpty a paid up member in the Royal Healthcare Scheme?
If Humpty Dumpty had sufficient faith would he have come back together?

Life is life, and the church itself is only a part of it.
If only the church was in its rightful place,
maybe Humpty would not have had a wall to fall from in the first place.
Or if the wall had not been so high
his fall would not not have been so severe!

The Cover Illustration is by Arthur Pateman
Copyright Mike Lowe 1995
First Impression September 1995
ISSN 0144-171 X
ISBN 1 85174 298 0

1
Into the Community

Back to the Parish with a New Outlook

Returning to 'the regulars' (the parish clergy) after having spent five years in a theological college was a most challenging and demanding experience. My first impression of my new parish was that of a very strong community of faith, which in fact shared far greater certainties than I myself owned. I was encouraged by the strong mission overtones in the parish profile. However, once the door was opened and I entered into the parish, it was very interesting to see what 'missionary' and 'evangelistic' meant. I look back on these observations over the past four years and draw conclusions particularly in the light of Robert Warren's recent research into what makes a missionary congregation.[1]

Networking

One of my first priorities in the parish was to 'network' the community.[2] Networking is a process in which one contacts various circles of people and comes alongside them, talks to them, listens to them and seeks to discover the various agendas owned by different groups. I visited all the local church leaders in the community who would give me an hour. I sat for many hours with them. I set aside one hour for each member of the PCC, following through a set of prepared questions on 'What is the mission of the church?' I also visited all the representatives of different interests in the community, meeting them to establish a relationship with them. I walked the bounds of the parish and prayed up and down the different streets of the parish. This process of networking is not only something of great value for the immediate but also builds up lots of contacts for the coming months and years. In networking the community, I kept hearing the same story, which somewhat disturbed me. I was to discover that the church had a very bad image in the wider community. This image was even at times a hostile one to the church. I heard many stories of hurt and rejection that really saddened me. I was sure that the bad image that the church had in the community was not altogether deserved.

---

1 Robert Warren, *Building Missionary Congregations*, (Board of Mission Occasional Paper No 4, London: Church House Publishing, 1995).
2 For further information on networking see Raymond Bakke, *The Urban Christian*, (Eastbourne: MARC Europe, 1987).

The Church with Walls

A couple of months into my ministry, I fed back to the PCC the things I had been discovering. They also were concerned to hear of the negative image that the church generally had in the wider community. In response to our discussion, they were pleased to agree to the proposal that a Media Committee should be appointed which would look at this question. The Media Committee should seek to ascertain why the church had got such a bad image and what action could be taken to rectify anything that was misunderstood. The Committee would be responsible for bringing back recommendations to the PCC on how to proceed. The Committee met for three years and consisted of the Vicar, four PCC members and three co-opted church members who were themselves involved in the media.

The Committee met, chaired by one of our lay people, a local headmaster. After spending time in prayer and preparation, we moved into the issues before us. We worked out our aims and objectives to submit them to the PCC, so that they would know what we were seeking to achieve and would have an opportunity to support it or not at a later date.

The Aim: To present the church in a meaningful manner to the community.
The Objectives:
1) To have a clear strategy for presenting the church in the media.
2) To overhaul our written materials in general.
3) To develop a positive and caring attitude through the occasional offices.
4) To explore the possibility of visual displays of church activities in the community.
5) To release the resources of the church to the wider community.
6) To provide promotional material.

It was agreed from the start that any effort that attempted to change the image of the church must embrace the whole range of our activities and literature. We had to admit that as a church we had excellent facilities in our campus, and yet our contact with the community was minimal. The decision was clearly made that we must not only go out into the community, but we must seek to bring the community into our church and campus.[3]

Talking to Those Outside

The first practical decision taken was to undertake some market research into the needs of the community, how it perceived the church and how it might respond to approaches made by us. A number of questionnaires were gathered together to consider their usefulness for our own particular task.

---

3   See Anne Coomes and Andy Radford, *How to Promote Your Church*, (London: Church House Publishing, 1995).

One produced by YWAM was adopted and adapted for our own particular needs.[4] This questionnaire was used throughout the community in different ways. Each of our Area Fellowship Groups was asked to visit a number of houses at random down selected streets. The over-18 group were invited to go on the streets and get the questions answered, outside the local Post Office and main supermarket. This gave us cause not only for concern but for encouragement, and led us to target certain areas as part of our mission. So the Committee had to begin a theological task and ask some basic questions:
1) To whom does the church belong? Various solutions were offered— PCC, Diocese, members, Marple, God, others.
2) What model of ministry are we applying? We looked especially at the servant ministry of Jesus as seen in Mark 10.45. What patterns are we following? Mark 2.13-17, Mark 13.1-2, 32-37, Galatians 6.10.
3) What is the relationship between the church and the kingdom?
4) How does the doctrine of creation address us in a rightful concern and responsibility for all humanity?
5) How do we see this working out in practice in our own situation?

The Press Officer

The aims and objectives of the Media Committee were presented to the PCC for their approval. We also shared some of our preliminary thinking and sought their insights and impressions. The question of appointing a Press Officer was raised, and the Media Committee was given the task of writing a job description for such a person and seeking to appoint somebody. Having advertised the opportunity in our weekly news-sheet, a very suitable applicant came forward and was quickly in place. The early work of contacting all the local press was accomplished and the first press release was carried by most of the local papers. We have since then kept up a barrage of press releases on our events, seeking to give a positive image of the activities of the church. We realized that we could not wait for the press to discover what we were doing and come to look at us; it was up to us to approach them and let them know. We also started to offer photographs for their periodicals. Since then we have made the front page on a number of occasions and frequently get reported within the covers of the local 'freebies.'

Clearly, the Committee was now considering more than just the media. The more cynical might call it 'the Vicar's think tank' and see it as his way of getting some of his own ideas onto the agenda as quickly as possible. The Committee was really addressing the mission of the church, seeking to work it out more fully and meaningfully in our own particular context of Marple.

---

4   Youth with a Mission Questionnaire, (YWAM, 13 Highfield Oval, Ambrose Lane, Harpenden, Herts AL5 4BX).

2
Vision and Planting

The Logo

The church logo appears on the front cover of this book. The choice of a logo in the Media Committee was a crucial decision. We decided that we could only find the right logo through much prayer and waiting upon God. It was during one session of prayer and waiting upon God that we did get the picture that has given the basis for the logo. Underneath are the hands of God, giving security to the church and making sure that no-one falls from the safety of those hands. The people are gathered around the cross, as that is at the very heart of the Christian gospel. Some of the people are in praise, others are just standing. Some are short, some are tall—there is the intention that there should be variety. Although there is a crowd around the cross, there is still a path that goes right to the foot of the cross which is open for anyone who wants to join us. We wrestled with the words that were to go with the logo for a long time. The conviction at the end of the day was the right words were—'HE CARES FOR ALL.' In this we felt that we were sending out a clear message of inclusiveness. This was the direction in which we wanted the church to go and this is what we wanted people to hear and see whenever our logo was seen. It was the intention that this parish logo should appear on all our literature, all our notice boards and be a key to what we stood for. In many ways it has become the vision statement for the parish. We do have two daughter churches—a church plant and a Victorian Mission Church—and it was important that the logo could also be used for them, so we avoided actually putting on it the name of the parish church. We really do believe that this logo was not our own invention or creation, but it was given and received from God in prayer. As a church we believe in the practise of the gifts of the Spirit. We have found over the years that the pictures God has given us in prayer have been very important and significant in giving us new direction. I do believe now that the logo we received and worked out has been of far more significance and importance in achieving our ends than ever we realized at first.

Identity

The basic ideas were communicated to a local artist who had recently become a Christian. We asked him to work on the basis of the picture described. He came up with some ideas which were not quite right, and we had to go back to him and ask him to redo his work. This he did gladly and the end product was exactly what we believed God had given us and we rejoiced in it. This logo now appears on everything that we publish and on every advertisement and hoarding. For instance, it is now on our new noticeboard which has been completely redone, and the logo stands there with the clear words next to it—'Welcome to your parish church'—the borders done in green and gold, which itself conveys a message. The logo appears on all our stationery, on our leaflets for the occasional offices, on evangelistic tracts and on our quarterly bulletin which goes out to every home in the parish. Over a period of three years we have clearly established our identity. This communicates to people that we value them and we include them in the life of the church. There is a place for them and we welcome them to find that place and to share with us the good things that we believe are to be found in Jesus Christ.

The logo in a very definite way expresses our vision statement for the parish—'HE CARES FOR ALL.' There is a place for you here. We want to come to you—please do come to us. The vision statement was worked out into a mission statement, with a very clear programme of commitment for the remaining years of the Decade of Evangelism. This was presented to the Annual Meeting of the church. It was initially well received and there was a lot of encouragement that we had such a positive direction. The proposal that we actually look for a further full-time member of staff to take the church out into the community was welcomed. We started the process of working out the details of the post and how this person should be engaged. He has now been on the staff for three years, and is about to leave to be ordained into a first curacy. His main brief was 'To take the church out into the community.' The three target areas identified were:

1) the local schools (5 primary, 1 comprehensive and 1 sixth form college),
2) the several residential homes for the elderly, and
3) pioneer our next church plant.

We already had one church plant, which was quite young and at that time flourishing. There were at least two other areas in the parish designated as suitable areas for church plants, and the mission statement included targeting both those areas for church plants in the years remaining in the Decade of Evangelism. The work of the Lay Curate in this outreach has been very much blessed, particularly in the schools work. He has quickly become established as a schools worker in all the seven educational institutions. He is involved in taking assemblies and R.E. lessons, Personal and Social Education, and in National Curriculum development of religious education. He is also seen as a friend and confidant of many of the staff who work in our town. This taking All Saints out into the schools, and the message of Jesus, has been a very significant move and we believe will bear fruit in the years to come, as well as the immediate fruit in families realizing that the church is concerned for their children. This has naturally developed in an increase of our Youth Work and the establishing of an annual Holiday Club in the last week of the summer holidays.

The full Mission Statement is given below.

THE PARISH OF MARPLE
ALL SAINTS/ST PAULS/CROSS LANE FELLOWSHIP
MISSION STATEMENT: SHARING THE VISION

VISION
- We look to God for revival
- We aim to see our membership at least double during this Decade of Evangelism

Current Normal Sunday Attendance: 400—286 Adults 114 Children
TARGET: Sunday Attendance: 800 —572 Adults 228 Children

STRATEGY:
- a) Intercessory prayer
- b) Church Planting
- c) Strategic outreach to particular grops
- d) Consolidation of present initiatives

a) INTERCESSORY PRAYER:
- To provide support for corporate and private prayer
- To establish well defined groups of intercessors

b) CHURCH PLANTING. Strategy for the next five years:
- Second Plant 1994/5
- Third Plant 1996/7

c) STRATEGIC OUTREACH. Getting into the community:
- Men's Outreach: Pub work/use of secular buildings
- Teenagers: get into youth culture
- Pastoral Care Team: lonely/sick/bereaved/unemployed/housebound

d) CONSOLIDATION
- Playgroup/Toddlers/Art Group
- Ladies: Lunchbreak and Christian Viewpoint

- Evaluation of Strines Mission Church
- *Impact* Broadsheet
- 6.30pm Service Steering Committee
- Social Committee

We aim to do this in partnership with all other churches in Marple that can share the same vision.

LEADERSHIP NEEDS: in order to be able to tackle this task we will need to increase our full time staff. I propose that we look for a full time appointment for the Autumn to head up the Church Planting Strategy, with a real commitment to get us off the hill and into the community. Please prayerfully consider this, asking the Lord to make clear whether this is his calling.

Intercessory Prayer

The commitment to prayer was seen as key, and we made sure that there was some good teaching given to the Fellowship:
1) through sermon series
2) through Area Fellowship Groups study material
3) through recommended books.

This, of course, is something every church has to come back to again and again. It was on intercessory prayer that we were focussing. We now have a defined set of intercessors who are willing to take on a prayer subject for twenty-one days (Daniel 10.13), and really look to God to bless, seeing a break-through in a particular area of the spiritual battle.

Church Planting

The strategy of church planting also speaks very clearly of a church with no walls. Church planting is a basic evangelistic outreach, taking the church to where people are, rather than expecting them to come to where we are. The first church plant here was done in a non-book culture of mainly council housing. The location chosen was the refectory at the local sixth form/FE college which was made available to us. The college is a community college in that it seeks not just to have sixth-formers in and out through the day, but many adults on a huge range of courses. The refectory was seen as a neutral place where people could come with absolutely no threat, and find something for themselves on their own terms. Each Sunday morning the refectory is converted into a worship centre by the careful use of chairs, a table, banners, PA equipment and overhead projector screen. We do not use any books at all in the plant—everything is on the acetates.

Positive or Negative?

Often in a neighbouring hall a drama class will be working, or a band or a dance class. Sometimes there is a car boot sale in the large car parks around the college. In some ways one feels vulnerable as a church meeting in this context, with so much glass and so much access from outside and so many activities going on. However, surely this is what a church should be if it has a commitment to being a church without walls. In our beautiful Victorian parish church, we are safely ensconced behind high stone walls with beautiful stained glass. I do not wish at all in any way to deride such a building—it is a magnificent place for worship. However, it does have its negatives, and one of those is the inaccessibility to many who have never been 'churched.' I still wonder at the difficulty it is for an unchurched person to actually walk through the normal portal of a Victorian building. If the average Christian was invited to go into a betting shop and place a bet, he or she would find the same difficulty, I am sure, that the unchurched person does in entering into one of our buildings. Where do I go and where do I sit—what do I do with these books—where do I pay my money? Certainly with a church plant you do remove much of that problem and give people a greater opportunity to come into the fellowship of Christians. However, it has been our discovery that there are always a certain number who do not consider it is a proper church! There is the evidence of people becoming new Christians, and lapsed Christians coming back to the faith, through the work of the church plant.

Second Plant

The second plant is planned for an area of middle class housing with quite high mobility, but in a clearly defined area with absolutely no church presence. The community of approximately 1500 people can be most effectively reached by a church presence immediately amongst them. So far a prayer cell has been working in the area for a year. It has not only met to pray and worship in the area, but it has done its prayer walks. It has also done demographic studies, and has conducted questionnaires around the area, finding out what people are interested in and their willingness to participate in such a project. However, it has not been easy for the mother church to accept the possibility of a further church plant, and that is some real pain we are working through at the present time.

Church planting is not without its difficulties and a good discussion of it is found in the bishop's report *Breaking New Ground*, together with George Lings' commentary on it in the Grove Evangelism series.[5]

---

[5] *Breaking New Ground*, (G.S.1099, London: Church House Publishing); George Lings *New Ground in Church Planting* (Grove Evangelism Series 27, Bramcote: Grove, 1994).

3
Strategic Outreach

Jesus commended the scribe who had been trained for the kingdom, in that he was like the master of the house who brought out of his treasure what is new and what is old. This is particularly true in this section of the mission statement. There is an intention to hold together the old and the new. The goal of at least doubling our numbers during the Decade of Evangelism was presented as both realistic and achievable. The strategy to achieve this was already outlined in prayer and church planting, but now worked out in specific outreaches and a consolidation of existing ones. The mission statement was generally well received at the Annual General Meeting. However, it was to take many months before it became widely owned and the will was there to see it implemented. The process of change is slow in the institution of the church. We discovered that we needed to find new ways of being the PCC. Change, even when it is clearly for the good—and not everyone felt that was necessarily the case in this instance—is painful. The degree of change required is still a constant factor in the life of the church, and in some ways inhibits numerical growth.

Strategic outreach was seen as necessary in three key areas in getting into the community:
1) outreach particularly to men
2) teenagers and their youth culture
3) pastoral care.

Men

After a half night of prayer, we made the commitment to have a strategic outreach to men in the community. The basic idea was not so much as to persuade men to come in and join us in the church, but to go out to where they were and be alongside them. This meant that a lot of our outreach was going to be into secular places where men meet, and that involved us going into pubs and clubs, buildings where men are to be found. This has been a successful outreach and has enabled quite a few men to come into the fellowship of the church. We also set up dinners and special events involving work and the workplace, seeking to engage men on their own ground.

Considerable pastoral care was taking place within the fellowship. However it was decided that we did need a thorough review. In doing this we established the resources already in place and sought to fill in gaps as they appeared. The intention was to offer first to the fellowship, but then to the wider community, an established pattern of pastoral care. This exercise was done quite thoroughly by a working group and we now have a central resource of pastoral care for lonely, sick, bereaved, unemployed and housebound. Along with this we have started to take Communion to the house-bound, by extension. The Bishop has agreed to license six of our lay people to help in this process. We now take fifty Communions out each month to those who are unable to come and join us here in the church building. As we say to them when we visit them, 'If you are unable to come to the church, then the church must come to you.'

Teenagers

The third strand of this strategic outreach was reaching out to young people. We already had an established youth work which was the envy of many churches. However, we were very conscious that we were not getting into the youth culture and we were only reaching a certain sector of young people. We did not succeed in making any real progress with this at all for two years. It was then that it was given to us as a gift. There is in Manchester a group called 'The Message' who have a ministry working in schools and youth places through cross-cultural media.[6] They asked if they could come to Marple, and we welcomed them. They did a very successful visit to the local Comprehensive School and conducted an alternative service in our church building at the end of the week. We now have built upon that and have our own alternative service on a regular basis for young people. These services usually include loud music, flashing lights, video production and messages in rap and other contemporary media. We now not only have a worker who goes out into the schools to where the children are, but we are getting the children coming into our building for their own service. This raises all the questions of integration and crossing the boundaries between the different congregations who now meet within the same building. However, it is a great joy to all that a significant number of young people who would never have darkened the doors of our church now feel free to come to us for that particular service.

Consolidation

Under the consolidation we identified those evangelistic outreaches that we already had into the community and sought to evaluate and build on them. As you can see from the mission statement, there is a list of several different projects. Progress has been made on each of these.

The *Impact* broadsheet is the name of our parish journal. Prior to this process it consisted of a series of sheets stapled together as an in-house document. We have replaced this with an A4 broad-sheet which is produced quar-

---

[6] Message to Schools Trust, Vicarage Gardens, Eaton Close, Cheadle Hume SK8 5EU. Telephone: 0161 486 6878.

terly and circulated free to the whole parish. The aim of the journal is evangelistic, but in a very open way. Many of the articles are open-ended and of local interest. We always seek to carry some item of local history and always try and cover any particular community events that have happened or are imminent. We seek to have a good range of photographs portraying the church in a very positive image, making sure they include plenty with young people and children enjoying themselves. The front page is devoted to a specific subject and has an editorial comment. Inside pages are evenly divided into church matters and community matters. We often run a specific article on one of the groups within the community, such as the Scouts. The back page is largely given over to children and young people, and it also includes details of 'hatchings, matchings, and dispatching.' The overall message of the Impact broad-sheet is that of our logo—'HE CARES FOR ALL.' We wish to communicate this message right through the parish to every home. We want to communicate the message that as the local church we are there for them and are interested in them, and want them to be interested in us. The *Impact* broad-sheet has reached a high standard of professionalism with the use of desk top publishing and laser printing.

The Church on the Hill

The church, as I have already said earlier, is located somewhat away from the centre of the community, and not all that easy to find, even though it is on 'Church Lane.' We approached the local council about sign-posting from the main street; they were somewhat reluctant to oblige. However, with persistence and by lobbying councillors, sign-posting was erected to point the way up the hill to the church. We also felt it was good to draw attention to the church by flood-lighting, both the West End and the Tower, at night time. This to some seems a waste of money, but it means the buildings stand out clearly and can be seen right through the town.

The climax of the Media Committee's work was the planning and organising, which took over a year, of an open weekend for the church in the summer of 1994. The vision was for a festival incorporating the whole weekend, which would put the whole life of the church on open view to the community and make a major invitation for the community to visit us and see what is going on here in the most non-threatening way. We were sending out the message to find out whether our image had changed and people would feel attracted and want to come and see.

All Saints Alive

We entitled the weekend 'All Saints Alive' and subtitled it 'a fiesta of fun, flowers and festivities.' With a marquee in our paddock and events going on throughout the church grounds as well as in the church building, we had a splendid weekend. There were flowers and other exhibitions throughout the building. There was food, there was dance, there was music, there were bouncy castles, there were art exhibitions, there was face painting—there was much going on.

The Tract

The Saturday evening came to an end with a large barbecue, where we were entertained by a Christian drama group who did a rock presentation. It was a wonderful weekend, did us all a power of good and certainly lifted our image in the community. One interesting story from that weekend was that the local bus run, which goes past the gate of the church paddock, actually decided to make it a bus stop for the day. Each time the driver went by he simply said to the passengers, 'They're having a good time here today—anyone want to get off and join them?' In actual fact people did get off the bus and came across to join us on our open day. One of the things we prepared for the open day was a very attractive tract which we produced along with 'Tell It' of Edinburgh. This tract sought to capture something of the beauty of Marple, something of its history and its background, along with a clear Christian gospel message. It was a most effective way of presenting the Christian message to people who came onto the campus.[7]

Spiritual Warfare

I would not want to finish this section of this chapter without stressing the first and underlying element of our strategy, and that was intercessory prayer. All these things have been done very much in the context and covering of intercessory prayer. For example, on the night before the open weekend, the staff team (seven of us) met and prayed and 'prayer-walked' right round our campus (about 5 acres) and we covered it in prayer and we specifically prayed and covered each entrance to the whole campus. It is so important to be reminded at all times that we are in a spiritual battle and that we do need to wage war in the heavenly places and find the victory of that prayer covering us in all outreach. As we sought to take the church into the community and bring the community into the church, we were very conscious of the need for prayer at every level.

---

[7] The Marple Tract, *Yesterday Today Forever*, (Tell It, 8 Noble Place, Edinburgh EH6 8AY). For a free sample send a SAE to 155 Church Lane, Marple, Stockport SK8 7LD.

4
A Theological Reflection

I have told you this story as it happened—an unfolding journey. Much of it was uncharted—a journey of faith. We are moving towards a model of church life which is a break with the past.

The present state of the church is described by Jose Comblin (*Being Human*, p 26), 'Most of us still live in the refuge of our parishes, which are more the relics of an antiquated Christianity than the first fruits of a new people won for Christ, in the midst of today's world.' Robert Warren, the National Officer for Evangelism of the Church of England's Board of Mission, has rightly challenged the complacent pastoral mode the church finds itself in, even half-way through this special decade. He also exposes the hard-working activists who try to make the present mode run in a higher gear! He sees the need for the church to find a new way of being the church in order that ultimately it might be transformed into a missionary congregation. Robert Warren argues for a new way of the church being the church. This is the most important thing to do before any action is considered. We need to re-examine our spirituality and if necessary refocus it, that it should be the basis of our motivation. Spirituality is very much an in-word in both the secular and faith situations. However, it must not be jettisoned because of that, since it holds the key to what it means for us to be the church. Robert Warren defines spirituality as 'our understanding and experience of how encounter with God takes place and how such an encounter is sustained.'

The Heart of the Matter

This 'heart' is where urgent attention is required. If only we can identify and own what is essential to our well-being and jettison the unhelpful baggage that we have accumulated. Europe is in a social cultural vacuum, and the church has today a unique opportunity to contribute to society. But we have to ask the questions: 1) have we the vision? and 2) are we willing to pay the cost of the change that is required? The movement that is required, according to Robert Warren, is from:

Church = Building + Priest + Stipend

to:

Church = Community + Faith + Action

This new formula demands a complete reorientation of our thinking of what is means to be God's people and to be fully engaged in God's world.

The traditional model of being evangelistic is that of a castle on a hill from which infrequent forays are made into the wider neighbourhood in order at least to save some! Those who are saved are brought up the hill to the castle and given the security of the high walls that protect. This could well be understood as an overstatement of this method of evangelism and in some ways one could commend the church that it cared sufficiently to go out on such ventures of faith. However, this is not the church without walls that is going to go out into the community to see the community changed and the church renewed.

The traditional images of the witnessing church as salt and light speak of the influence that we must have on society. The problem is that the church has become to many a symbol of irrelevance. In our leisure society, with its 'pick and mix' attitude to values, those who call themselves Christians are entitled to have their bit of religion, but of course the Christian faith is about life. It is not just about a hobby that fits in with a lot of other things in a busy week.

All Saints Church, Marple is geographically in a situation which fits with that traditional form of evangelism that can be so easily exposed as inadequate. We are on a hill and have very fine buildings with strong walls. Sometimes little boys come up and throw stones through our stained glass windows and run away. I guess some would comment that if we did live in the midst of the community and we were surrounded by people, we would probably have to board up our stained glass windows! But is this because the church is not recognized since it has failed to be the church and has ended up as rather a quaint alien institution that speaks of values of another day? In taking down the walls of the church we seek to be inclusive, not to 'baptize' everything indiscriminately, as clearly that which is bad needs to be recognized and opposed. However, there is much good that we can and should baptize and affirm.

Church members have found it quite difficult to adjust to the new values which have been brought in through our work here in Marple. I can hear them often saying it was much simpler before this all began, when we knew that some were out and some were in. Indeed the strength of the previous policy is a strong community of faith, but its weakness is the alienation it gives to others who are at a further place. When we talk of pilgrimage, of journey, we need to help people see that there are many different places on that journey. It is important to see there is not just one pen where the sheep have arrived and need to be secured. Sometimes one asks the question, 'why do they need to be secure?'—it is almost as if there is a fear that they might escape!

I would like to quote at length from a recent missionary prayer letter from CMS missionary partners in Sudan. I quote from the letter of Andy and Sue Wheeler, No 42 dated April 1995:

A THEOLOGICAL REFLECTION

'In Yambio, where I recently attended the NSCC General Assembly, something quite different is happening. I referred in a previous letter to the Church's concern in Yambio at how young people were losing their traditional culture, throwing over traditional moral values and no longer knew the traditional stories and history of their people. The Episcopal Church has started a museum of traditional artefacts. On this visit, following the General Assembly, we were given a performance of traditional dances. The first preserved a dance by boys about to be circumcised. The second, however, was a dance by two traditional diviners/healers—who in the course of their dance endeavoured to identify people who were the source of conflict or disease in the community. The dance was played for laughs, but there was an edginess in the atmosphere, and a touch of fear in the audience whenever one of the diviners came too close. The startling thing for me was that the drummers for the two dances were pastors and one of the two "diviners" was also a pastor.

Afterwards I asked one of the pastors what lay behind the pastors' involvement with such dances. He said that it was part of the Church's concern to preserve the heritage of the past before it disappeared. "Our culture," he said, "is a gift from God—we must preserve what is good in it, whilst not being afraid to reject what is bad." "So, what about the diviners' dance?" I asked. "We need to remember our past and preserve the authentic songs and dances—but we also need to take the fear and seriousness out of it. That is why we make it humorous."

Watching the audience, I was less certain that the fear had been "exorcized." And from the diviners' dance we went straight into church for a thanksgiving service for the Assembly. My mind was reeling—all the way through what seemed an endless list of welcomes and greetings, in which virtually everyone present, including the *imam*, was welcomed and given a few moments to speak.

Then slowly my mind put it together—the extraordinary inclusiveness of Africa—an inclusiveness that even takes in cultural oddballs like me. It seems that nothing is excluded from the African awareness of reality, not even the dark, fearful and ambiguous. And no-one is excluded from the community, not the diviner and not the *imam*, as the interminable welcomes in the church had demonstrated. Everything and everyone had its place. That is not to say that everything has the same or an equal place. The dark and evil things have their definite and controlled place in the shadows at the periphery. Those things that are good and true find their way to the centre. Sue and I had often noticed in the past that no matter how great someone's crimes or offences against the community might be, relationships were never totally severed. There was always a place, always a way back. No situation was irredeemable.

For the moment, the situation amongst the Bor Dinka seems to be different. So devastating has been the war, so radically have the foundations been shaken, that it appears a total break with the past has been made. Can African people sustain such separation from their ancestors, their psychological and communal roots? And what relationship will they establish with the God of Jesus, the God of Abraham, Isaac and Jacob? How will the inclusive circle be maintained?

The implications of this are many. For one, the Sudanese Church will always be "a church without walls"—as it often literally is. There is a spectrum of faith—from those at the centre who have a deep personal and transforming faith in Christ, through those whose faith is yet uncertain, through those who are still journeying towards faith, and on out to those who as yet acknowledge no Christian faith at all (like the *imam* and the diviner). Positively, the possibility is always there of people throughout the spectrum being drawn closer to Christ. Negatively, the meaning of the word "Christian" can become extremely vague if those at the centre lose the fire of the gospel and cease to attract those at the periphery to the centre. The movement will then flow the other way, away from the gospel, away from faith.'[8]

In this parable from Africa we see something of the challenge of a church without walls, and a church that is seriously seeking to be part of its culture and address the needs of its people. I am sure there will be bells ringing in many people's minds as they hear something of Andy's experience, particularly with the diviners. However, I do not believe we should be always on the defensive (always concerned with avoiding pollution)—we should be rather on the offensive. I often draw people's attention to 1 John 4.4 where the teaching on testing the spirits is given by John:

'Little children, you are from God and have conquered them. For the one who is in you is greater than the one who is in the world.'

The inclusiveness that we see in this story from Africa gives us a challenge and an invitation to take seriously the inclusiveness that we should, I believe, be exploring in our own culture. As a young Christian, I was always very troubled by the goodness I found outside the church. I thank God now that my understanding of his purposes, his kingdom and the work of his Spirit, is such that I rejoice in the goodness I find outside the church. I am now able to understand it theologically in the context of his purposes. If only Christians were more welcoming and more positive about such good-

---

[8] CMS Prayer Letter, Church Missionary Society, 157 Waterloo Road, London SE1 8UU.

ness, that would be a good start.

The Spirit of God is refreshing his church at the present time. We see this particularly in what has been labelled the 'Toronto blessing.' It is good in some sense to label it in such a way that it recognizes a definite incarnational point when this blessing was given in a particular place. However, now it is seen recurring in places all over the world, and is particularly strongly in the United Kingdom. It is estimated that around 4,000 churches have been affected by this new work of the Spirit of of God. In making that statement I realize that there are many Christian brothers and sisters who have decided that it is not of God. I guess on that we have to disagree. It seems to me that the most important thing that is happening is not the phenomena, although they are quite fascinating, it is the deeper sense of the presence of God that the church is gaining. It is in this whole area of spirituality, of knowing the nearer presence, the imminence of God, of being sure of God's love and purposes that the church is being refreshed and is being renewed in a new way. As the heart of the church grows stronger then the church is in a better place to become a missionary congregation. When the centre is secure in the love of God and the knowledge of his purposes, then there is the willingness to change, there is the willingness to do things differently and to move out into real worship and service in the community.

I would not like to suggest that this whole journey is what we have been experiencing at All Saints, but we have been doing so at least in part. The greatest compliment I believe anyone has ever paid me, was that of a Methodist minister introducing me to a new Anglican vicar in his parish, who said, 'Mike—he's a kingdom man.' I do really believe that we need to be committed to the issues of the kingdom rather than the issues of the church. The debate of the relationship of the church to the kingdom continues. I see the church as being both a sacrament and a signpost to the kingdom. However, at times, maybe more often than we would like to admit, it has been a bad sacrament and a bad signpost. The fact of the incarnation means that the church has to become, as it has done, an institution. As Robert Warren rightly points out, people today do not function well in institutions. They function far better in networks.

Just as all of us are on a journey, even so the local church is on a journey. All Saints, Marple is on a journey and it has shared a little of that journey with you in this Grove booklet—shared it through the eyes of its vicar. It would be interesting if the same journey could be described through the eyes of a number of different people in the congregation. I am sure there would be some who would argue that they have just become uncomfortable and have not understand why and felt a lot more secure when things were not so open. I believe one of the interesting factors that has come from this process is that regular church members have become less regular. It is almost as if they have been given permission not to be at every service and not even to feel a compulsion to be even there every Sunday. This of course lowers one's normal Sunday attendance and does not look good in statistics. However, it does give space in the congregation for new people to come in and occupy those seats. And whilst your church members are out in the community, they have the opportunity to be salt and light, an opportunity they do not have within the walls of the church building.

It is important to recognize that any change causes pain, and that a lot of pastoral care is required to support and help the members of the church as a process like this evolves. It does seem that people need things explained again and again and in different ways. If people can capture something of the reason for the changes, then they start to be more prepared to cope with them. However, I am not sure, having said this, that all those in my church with its different congregations, would necessarily agree with me.

Epilogue

Humpty Dumpty had a fragile shell, and when he fell off the wall he was permanently damaged. There is a great fragility in society today at all levels. The church itself has been exposed in its own weakness. There is a great need for the church to to regain its essential spirituality and to own it. It is from this strength, and this strength alone, that we can be the church of Jesus Christ without fear. After all, it is his church and his world.

William Temple has often been quoted, 'The Church is the only body that exists primarily for the benefit of those who are not its members.' However often this has been highlighted, we still do not seem to have incarnated this essential insight.

Emil Brunner once said, 'The church exists for mission as fire exists for burning.' The church that is truly the church does not need walls. If the fire at the centre is burning brightly, the flow will always be from the periphery to the heart. I make my final plea. What are the walls in place for—to keep the sheep in or to keep the goats out? Let us pull down those walls for the many Humpty Dumpties in our broken fragmented world who desperately need the good news of Jesus Christ.

> 'The Spirit of the Lord is on me because He has anointed me to preach good news to the poor. He sent me to proclaim freedom for the prisoners and recovery of sight for the blind, to release the oppressed, to proclaim the year of the Lord's favour.' Luke 4.18-19 (NIV).